STANDARDS-BASED COUNSELING IN THE MIDDLE SCHOOL

By

Mary Ellen Davis

ISBN: 1-4033-1086-6 (e-book)
ISBN: 1-4033-1087-4 (Paperback)
ISBN: 1-4033-3895-7 (Dustjacket)

This book is printed on acid free paper.

1stBooks - rev. 01/15/03

To the middle and high school students

who touched my life

during my thirty-seven years of

teaching and counseling.

To LeNorris and Tarik

Acknowledgements

I am grateful to the following people for their encouragement and assistance:

The Principal of West Middle School, the counseling department staff, the faculty, support service providers, and the PTSA. I especially thank the head counselor for always making herself available to ask the critical questions, give feedback and offer assistance.

Dr. Patricia Nellor Wickwire, Editor of the California Association for Counseling and Development Journal, you for inviting me to attend your Writing Workshop. Thank you encouraging me to write my first article for the Journal, and for your guidance and critical editing.

Dr. Marcellet Henry, [Retired] State Department of Education Sacramento, and one of the founding members of the California Association for Multicultural Counseling (CAMC), a division of CACD, for encouraging and assisting me to write the history of CAMC.

Mary Ellen Rudden, former English teacher, for reading the draft of the manuscript and transforming it into a document worthy of publication.

Dr. Paul De Sena, Professor of Counselor Education, Loyola Marymount University, Los Angeles, for reading the manuscript, asking questions, making statements, and giving pointers, and encouraging me to finish it.

Dr. Elizabeth Van Dalsem, Professor Emeritus, San Francisco State University, for reading the manuscript, asking clarifying questions, making suggestions and corrections, and encouraging remarks.

Preface

During a discussion with the counseling staff about counseling programs, we took a serious look at our school counseling program. We realized that while we were working diligently performing our counseling duties, and supporting parents, teachers, and other support service providers, we needed to define our program in a way that explained what we do and how we do it to meet the needs of students. We began to close the gap by holding two all-day Saturday meetings to discuss the National Counseling Standards and determine how we could incorporate them into our counseling practices to improve student development in the academic, career, and personal/social areas.

We invited the principal to meet with us to share his input about our current counseling activities, and informed him of our plans. Next, we designed and showed a power point presentation to the faculty. We asked for their input as we shared and explained our counseling plans. Lastly, we showed the power point presentation to the school Parent, Teacher, and Student Association (PTSA) members and sought input from them. Both the faculty and the PTSA showed interest and offered support. Our presentations were well received. We enhanced our counseling program by incorporating Standard A of each of the three developmental areas—Academic, Career, and Personal/Social.

Contents

Chapter One

The mere imparting of information is not education. Above all things, the effort must result in making a person think and do for himself.

Carter G. Woodson

Overview of the National Standards for School Counseling Programs

In the past, school counseling often received marginal support and limited recognition from site administrators, district administrators, and members of the community. Regardless of the scant notice paid to the profession, its importance is obvious. School counselors, like teachers, are providers to our most important resource—our nation's children.

Recent national and state legislation support the profession. In the past few years, more attention has been given to developing strong, consistent school counseling programs. The American School Counselor Association's creation of the national counseling standards provide guidance and direction for delivering effective counseling services.

The American School Counselor Association, in its publications *Sharing the Vision: The National Standards for School Counseling Programs* (Campbell & Dahir, 1997) *and Vision into Action: Implementing the National*

Standards for School Counseling Programs (Dahir, Sheldon, & Valiga, 1998), has classified into specific standards all of the services school counselors have traditionally delivered. Armed with this clearly defined, understandable information, counselors can deliver a program in three broad areas of student development, which include all aspects of human development—academic, personal/social, and career.

In the article, Standards-Based Counseling in the Middle School (Davis, 2000), the following explanation details the need for trained counselors.

> Effective school counseling utilizes the special training of credentialed counselors and various counseling methods to deliver information and services. School counselors use the national counseling standards to assist students to learn and to apply the skills necessary to support continuing education and lifelong learning. The counseling standards guide the counseling program, including counselors, administrators, teachers, students, and parents, to focus on developmental competence. (p.49)

The national standards offer reasonable guidelines for developing and implementing school counseling programs. Armed with the clearly defined, easily understood information that is presented in the national standards, counselors can deliver an effective program in three broad areas of student development: academic, personal/social and career.

In *Sharing the Vision: The National Standards for School Counseling Programs,* Campbell and Dahir explain the national counseling standards and how they fit into the school instructional program. The national standards for counseling are designed to accomplish the following:

1. Create a framework for a national model for school counseling programs.
2. Identify the key components of a school-counseling model program.
3. Identify the knowledge and skills that all students should acquire as a result of the K-12 school counseling program.
4. ensure that school counseling programs are comprehensive in design and delivered in a systematic fashion to all students.
5. establish school counseling as an integral component of the academic mission of the educational system.
6. encourage equitable access to school counseling services for all students, provided by a credentialed school counselor. (p. 5).

Campbell and Dahir quote the American School Counselor Association on what a school counseling program should entail:

> A comprehensive school counseling program is developmental and systematic in nature, sequential, clearly defined, and accountable.
>
> It is jointly founded upon developmental psychology, educational philosophy, and counseling methodology (ASCA, 1994). The school counseling program is integral to the educational enterprise. The program is proactive and preventive in its focus … School counseling programs are developed by design, focusing on needs, interests, and issues related to the various stages of student growth. There are objectives, activities, special services, and expected outcomes, with an emphasis on helping students to learn more effectively and efficiently. (p. 9).

The national standards include information pertinent to all areas in the development and implementation of school counseling programs, including the vision, the mission, the rationale, and the goals and objectives.

The Vision of the School Counseling Program

The vision of the school counseling program is the delivery of counseling services to facilitate growth and development of the whole student (social, personal, emotional, physical, academic, cultural, and spiritual). Students will acquire and develop knowledge, attitudes, and skills that enable them to experience lifelong academic, career and personal/social development and career success.

The Mission of the School Counseling Program

Counselors are charged with the awesome mission of finding ways to empower students to view themselves as "miracles in progress." Their mission is to help students understand that personal power lies in their uniqueness, and in their educational development.

Students must come to see themselves not only as individuals, but also as members of a group, a class, a school, and a society. It is the counselor's mission to help students view their place in the world and to impart to them the connectedness of the human spirit by teaching what it means to accept, to respect, to appreciate, and to share with others. In so doing, counselors help students to understand and to respond in ways that promote both individual and communal achievement.

The Rationale for the School Counseling Program

The rationale for the school counseling program lies in its relationship to the instructional program. School counselors complement and supplement the instructional program by assessing students, teaching students to develop positive attitudes toward school, and monitoring students' academic progress. They work with students, staff, parents, teachers, and the community to maintain a school environment that removes barriers to learning.

School counselors know and understand the value of caring relationships. They help students develop positive attitudes and enjoy successful experiences by the following methods:

1. Encouraging students to think about, decide and act on issues related to academic achievement, personal/social skills development and future career choices.
2. Counseling students in problem solving.
3. Conducting personal student conferences.
4. Collaborating with teachers.
5. Arranging and facilitating student-teacher conferences.
6. Arranging and facilitating student-parent-teacher-support staff conferences.
7. Facilitating large group meetings.
8. Conducting small and large group instruction.
9. Making referrals to support providers.

The Goals and Objectives of the School Counseling Program

The primary goal of school counseling is to assist students in the learning process. In his Monograph, *Stating the Goals of Counseling*, Krumboltz (1966) makes the following observation:

> Recognizing that all children do not develop in a linear fashion, according to a certain timetable, there is intentional overlapping among grade levels (elementary, middle/junior high, and high school). The school counseling program reflects the progression of student development throughout the pre-K through grade 12 experience. (p.12).

Counselors use various strategies in working with and understanding the growth and development of students. Krumboltz (1966) gives a set of criteria for counseling goals:

> 1. The goals of counseling should be capable of being stated differently for each individual client.
> 2. The goals of counseling for each client should be compatible with, though not necessarily identical to, the values of his counselor.
> 3. The degree to which the goals of counseling are attained by each client should be observable. (p.5).

The objective of the school counseling program is to identify and support specific learning outcomes in the academic, personal/social, and career areas. Students are guided through discovery, understanding, and application. The acquisition of learning competencies will enable students to demonstrate knowledge, attitudes, and skills in each of these areas. Campbell and Dahir note the scope of the counselor's responsibilities:

> It is understood that mastery of basic skills facilitates the mastery of higher order skills in each area of development. The school counselor utilizes a variety of strategies, activities, delivery methods, and

resources to promote the desired student development. The school counselor's responsibilities include the design, organization, implementation, and coordination of the program. (p.11).

The Developmental Areas: Academic, Personal/Social, Career

The content standards for academic development guide the school counseling program to implement strategies and activities that will support and maximize student learning. Academic development includes the following:

1. Acquiring knowledge, attitudes, and skills which contribute to effective learning in school and across the life span
2. Employing strategies to achieve success in school
3. Understanding the relationship of academics to the world of work and the relationship of academics to life at home and in the community

The content standards for personal/social development guide the school counseling program to provide the foundation for personal and social growth as students progress through school and into adulthood. This will contribute to academic and career success as well as to the acquisition of knowledge, attitudes, and skills that help students do the following:

1. Understand and respect self and others
2. Acquire effective interpersonal skills
3. Understand safety and survival

The content standards for career development guide the school counseling program to provide the foundation for the acquisition of knowledge, attitudes, and skills that will enable students to make successful transitions from both school to the world of work and from job to job across the life span. Career development includes employment of strategies that will help students do the following:

1. Achieve future success and job satisfaction
2. Understand the relationship between personal qualities, education, training, and the world of work

The Components of the School Counseling Program

Counseling services are available to all students, and all students are made aware of the extent of counseling services provided at the school site.

The components of the school counseling program include personal, small-group, and large-group counseling and guidance activities. Within that framework, counselors provide the following services: consultation, coordination, case management, collaboration, and development and delivery of guidance curriculum.

Personal (one-on-one) counseling permits undisturbed sessions with the counselor. Students feel free to express their feelings and to explore ideas. They have the assurance that they will be met with concern and confidentiality.

Small-group counseling involves three to ten participants and permits students to discuss ideas to solve problems, and to share experiences and feelings with other members of the group. In small-group counseling sessions, the counselor can facilitate the building of relationships.

Large-group counseling includes a class or an entire grade level. The purpose is to disseminate information of common interest to the group.

Counselors, in addition to personal and group services, make referrals to specific professionals whenever a student's welfare is in jeopardy or when long-term services are needed.

Consultation services include arranging and participating in conferences and providing information and guidance. The counselor assists and supports parents, teachers, administrators, social service agencies, and medical personnel to work together more effectively.

In seeking equitable access to programs for all students and in facilitating student development, the school counselor coordinates and participates in activities that involve all who are relevant to the education and well-being of students.

The school counselor does case management by monitoring individual student progress and activities toward the achievement of desired outcomes in the academic, personal/social, and career aspects of human development.

In collaborating with teachers, the school counselor assesses the needs of students, evaluates program activities, and make changes to meet their needs.

In developing school guidance curriculum, the school counselor formulates goals and objectives and prepares educational activities directly related to the counseling standards. The curriculum might address specific concerns such as organizational skills; group relationships; study skills; social/life skills development; test taking; information pertinent to high school, college, and career development. Delivery may be in large and small groups directed by the school counselor or in the classroom directed by the teacher.

The counseling program is most effective with a manageable number of counselees. Campbell and Dahir give the ratio of 300 to 1 counselor as "manageable," but the ideal would be much lower. Currently, the ratio in California is 950-1.

The Role of the School Counselor

The school counselor's role is to complement and supplement the instructional program by supporting, teaching, and guiding students. The counselor's ultimate charge is to ensure that students have positive and healthy school experiences.

School counselors are credentialed and trained in specific areas and methods of delivery. The counselor is both an advocate for students and a professional caregiver who helps build relationships among students, staff, parents, and the community.

Counselors spend their work days and hours beyond providing such services as facilitating, guiding, teaching, case managing, and collaborating with school staff, parents/guardians, law enforcement, mental health workers, district-level staff, emergency community medical services, and personnel at other schools.

Concluding Statement

Students need counseling and guidance services to help them through the school years. Legislators, counselor educators, boards of education, and school-site principals are charged with the responsibility of mandating, training, and hiring credentialed counselors to serve all students. The critical national need for sound guidance makes counseling an educational priority.

Reprinted as adapted with permission from the CACD Journal, 2000. Vol. 20, pp. 49-54.

Chapter Two

Whatever we believe about ourselves and our ability comes true for us.

Susan L. Taylor

The Middle School Counselor: Skills and Qualities

Children between the ages of eleven and fourteen have their own special needs. This is the age group that is caught in the middle. Parents expect the school counselor to help their children through the often confusing and turbulent time of middle school. They expect the counselor to give them information, to answer their questions and to teach them how the school works. And, they expect the counselor to treat their children fairly.

The middle school counselor's personal qualities and professional skills are paramount in effectively engaging students, parents, colleagues, and members of the community. Experience, commitment, and a broad knowledge of techniques are relevant to success.

The ability of the counselor to demonstrate a caring spirit is essential when counseling middle school students. Acceptance by students of respect for their feelings and opinions, and parents' feelings of satisfaction is evidenced by the nurturing attitude of the school counselor.

Bennett (2000) in his doctoral dissertation, "*Self-perceptions of Support for the Professional Role of Language Pathologists in Public School Settings*," lists traits conducive to successful counseling. Although Bennett is referring to speech pathologists, the qualities he puts forth are applicable to anyone whose objective is to help people help themselves. According to Bennett, a successful counselor is one who:

1. Is service oriented and appreciates and values giving clients the support they need to develop and grow
2. Enjoys communication and interactions with others
3. Is psychologically astute and willing to look within one's self
4. Demonstrates flexibility
5. Enjoys learning
6. Values the scientific paradigm
7. Possesses a broad world perspective
8. Serves independently and values self-reliance
9. Is emotionally honest
10. Knows how to listen
11. Knows how to set limits
12. Possesses sensitivity in offering feedback
13. Prizes language at many levels
14. Prizes discipline and perseverance

The Middle School Counselor: Multifaceted Role

The multifaceted role of the middle school counselor has been either the best kept secret or among the most ignored areas of educational review (the author thinks the latter). It would be difficult to encapsulate a day in the life of a middle school counselor, but it would be safe to say that 90% of that day would involve responding to individual student needs.

The middle school counselor is an advocate who supports, teaches, and guides. In a support role, the middle school counselor facilitates appropriate class placement or appropriate curricular modifications. In a teaching role, the middle school counselor helps students become more mindful of their potential and confident of their abilities. In the role of guidance, the middle school counselor directs students to accept personal responsibility, and to set realistic goals.

In his brochure, "A Teacher Is," Trujillo (1988) writes about the teacher-student classroom relationship. The words he uses might easily apply to the counselor/counselee relationship. Adapting Trujillo's words, the middle school counselor is a professional who guides students toward lifelong learning and achievement through:

> Fastening: Helping students put even little things together.
> Supporting: Helping students explore the avenues of the mind.
> Conveying: Taking students places they have never been.
> Transmitting: Acting as a courier for information delivery.
> Securing: Supporting safety for all students.
> Bonding: Providing the glue that holds students together.
> Confiding: Developing relationships that engender trust.

The Middle School Counselor: Transacting the Business of Counseling

Middle school counseling service is serious business. There are rules and regulations to enforce, students to nurture, and students to calm. There is the teaching of right from wrong, and the changing of bad conduct into good.

There are children to mold, parents to please, and society's norms to validate.

Part of the middle school counselor's job is helping students understand and abide by various sets of rules—federal, state and city codes; school district policies; school and classroom rules—and maintain their individuality.

As the schools become more culturally diverse, the school counselor experiences greater challenges. A conflict may arise when regulations (even what are sometimes regarded as universal moral laws) are in opposition to a family's values. The counselor must be educated in and accept different cultural and religious values. The counselor must respect differences, and accept their importance to the student and family. The counselor must proceed with sensitivity and competence when a family asks that their own cultural or religious imperatives override specific codes or school rules.

In the publication "Culturally Competent Nursing Care," (Lipson, Dibble & Minarik, 1998) discuss the difference between cultural sensitivity and cultural competence. The following discussion applies equally to school counselors in their work with students of various cultures:

> …the advantage of "competence" over terms like sensitivity is that it implies not only awareness, but also the ability to intervene appropriately and effectively. Cultural competence … requires much more than simply acquiring knowledge about another ethnic/cultural group. (p. 1)

The acquisition of cultural information can be detrimental if used with counselees and parents without the knowledge of the culture, the skills, and the attitude necessary to deliver effective service. Lipson, Dibble & Minarik make the following statement about cultural information:

> Cultural information by itself can interfere with care if it is used in a cookbook manner and attempt to apply cultural "facts" indiscriminately to a person of a particular ethnic group. Cultural information can lead to stereotyping ... particularly by caregivers who lack self-awareness, are ethnocentric, or who fail to recognize variability within any cultural group. (p. 2)

Some regulations must be enforced regardless of cultural or religious objections, but others may be flexible. The counselor must be knowledgeable of what can be modified and what cannot, and educate parents as to both.

Responding to students is at the core of the middle school counselor's job. Working effectively takes skill, patience, and persistence. The responsibilities of the middle school counselor are great and the expectations of the community considerable.

Middle school counselors are trained in techniques and methods to meet different social and psychological needs. Such training might address a submissive student who feels alone and isolated or an aggressive student who feels his/her personal demands should prevail.

Disruptive attitudes and behaviors affect everyone—the individual, the classroom environment, the school, and society as a whole. Middle school counselors spend some time disciplining students for minor disturbances that can be handled in a short amount of time employing counseling and guidance strategies. The head counselor and the assistant principal handle major discipline problems.

To be effective, the middle school counselor must pay attention to even the smallest things, as small things can grow in significance and become intractable problems. There is mounting national concern that a general acquiescence to unacceptable behavior is one of the chief reasons for students' lack of educational achievement.

In an article about a research project in the Missouri schools, "Helping Seventh Graders Be Safe and Successful: A Statewide Study of the Impact of Comprehensive Guidance and Counseling Programs," Lapan, Gysbers, and Petroski (2001) states that

"Schools and school counselors in the United States today face a daunting array of challenges generated from profound social, cultural, and economic changes that occurred in the last half of the twentieth century and that will continue into the twenty-first century" (p. 320). Safety, as expressed in the article, is one of the main concerns of school staff, parents, and the community. "Keeping students safe has become a primary focus for everyone involved in America's schools. School counselors have an important role in promoting and maintaining student safety" (p.320).

Episodes of horrific school violence in the past few years have put the spotlight on the need for effective school counseling. It is believed by some people that society has become increasingly lax in curbing negative behavior. Some students have too often been led to believe that they can say whatever they want to say, do whatever they want to do, and act however they want to act, regardless of the impact such choices have on their own destinies and the destinies of those who must share their environment. In some school settings, a few students (five to ten percent of the student population) wear negative attitudes like neon signs to elicit adult reaction and to attract the attention of other students. Bad behavior can be popular. A student who exhibits negative behavior might garner the admiration of other students in much the same way a celebrity garners the admiration of fans.

It is a challenge to counsel those middle school students who defend their right to express thoughts and opinions in any manner they might choose. Such students refuse to see their own behavior as destructive. While they may express a loss of status and may feel devalued by what they consider disrespectful treatment from others, they do not see their own behavior in a similar light. This type of behavior demands additional resources. The counselor, the parent and the support staff seek help from other service providers, and from the medical and the mental health communities.

While most middle school students navigate the turbulence of physical and mental growth and development, the middle school counselor must impart to all students that restraint and self-control will enable them to perform more effectively and will enable them to enjoy positive experiences now and throughout their lives.

Although counselors are trained to facilitate conflict resolution and to provide crisis counseling, being effective with middle school students who exhibit continuous negative behavior can be fraught with problems. Hostility to authority can dominate, and attempts to counsel can provoke further anger. Hostile students may feel insulted when their opinions are questioned and may express indignation when asked to clarify statements or discuss solutions. They often feel justified in their actions and resent those who challenge the validity of what they see as righteous anger. Attempts to change such attitudes and behaviors in the middle school student may not be completely successful where maturity, self-awareness, and a sense of personal responsibility may be absent. However, the counselor doesn't give up nor give in. There are continuous efforts to help students help themselves. At this point, the counselor consults with the parent and other support personnel to assist the student to modify behavior.

Ruggiero (2000), in an article from The American Teacher, "*Bad behavior*: *confronting the views that hinder students' learning*," discusses research on oppositional attitudes that have implications for education. "Students' displays of rudeness and hostility are learned behavior traceable to the fallacious notion that emotional health depends on ventilating negative feelings." (p.46). According to Ruggiero, the following unhealthy attitudes prohibit learning:

> "Being myself makes self-discipline unnecessary." (p.15).
> "If I have high self-esteem, I will be successful." (p.16).
> "I have a right to my opinion, so my opinions are right." (p.45).
> "Expressing my negative feelings will relieve them." (p.46).
> "…the teacher's job is to entertain me." (p.47).

Ruggiero suggests that the origin of oppositional attitudes lies in "… mass culture, the ideas and values disseminated by the entertainment and communications media, (books, newspapers, magazines, popular music, radio, and television) and by the advertising industry" (p.12).

Shaw (2001) in his book Jack and Jill, Why They Kill, refers to students' knowledge of right and wrong and good and bad as 'moral intelligence' (p.31).

Since students cannot be held responsible for behaviors they have not learned, how does a middle school counselor proceed in helping students develop "moral intelligence"?

The underpinning of a value system lies in clear concepts of acceptable and unacceptable. When a rule is violated, the middle school counselor must first seek to determine whether the student understands right from wrong (as it pertains to a given situation) and then guide the student to change the inappropriate conduct into appropriate conduct by developing alternative behaviors to meet his needs.

Discipline and understanding do not necessarily work together. While consequences may be warranted, lasting change will not follow unless the student fully understands the rationale behind a rule and the relevance of the rule to his/her life. For these reasons, students must clearly understand the "why" as well as the "what."

Consequences for unacceptable behavior should make an impression and should be timely. Consequences need to be understood by the student as appropriate to the behavior in question. Efforts at changing negative behavior are counterproductive if the student sees the punishment or remedy as disproportionate to the offense.

Inasmuch as parents are partners in the education of their children, school counseling must be coupled with parental guidance. Parents must be respectfully informed of all negative behavior, and their help must be enlisted. Parent conferences frequently provide insight and give the counselor a starting point.

Counselors make a point of informing parents about positive things related to their children. Parents do not welcome phone calls or letters informing them of their child's unacceptable behavior. Hearing such news is painful. All parents want to hear positive things about their children and sometimes can react unhappily when told otherwise. Emotional reactions do not change the need to inform and engage parents, and should not deter teachers and counselors from involving them.

Many adults recall just a few decades ago when the types of negative behavior and language commonly expressed by today's youth were unthinkable. Obscene and violent language has slipped unchecked into the accepted vocabulary of today's middle school children. Based on more than twenty years of counseling middle and high school students and observing some students' interactions with peers and adults, it is becoming more and more obvious that respect for others and the acceptance of diversity are too often the exception rather than the rule.

All adults in the child's life are role models—good or bad. Children do as they see others do. Some values—common courtesy, good manners, polite speech—can be considered by some to be old-fashioned by today's standards. The values of past generations that embody the essence of being a good person, being a good citizen are unquestionably relevant. Adults must exhibit these values and virtues if they want to see them instilled in children. The way to teach right behavior and good conduct is by exemplifying it—modeling it.

Teaching good behavior involves creating an awareness of others and an awareness of whether one's personal actions are compatible with the rest of society. Teaching respect and acceptance of diversity will be successful only when practiced by the parent, the teacher, the school counselor, and other significant persons in students' lives. A student who learns to accept and to respect others will be more inclusive, more tolerant, and less inclined to engage in anti-social behavior.

An essential element in the middle school counselor's attempt to modify student behavior is active listening. The counselor listens actively to students and students are encouraged to listen actively to the counselor.

Each must be permitted to express their remarks respectfully. The counselor must remember that good listening allows one to hear more than the words that the student verbalizes.

Mackay (June 3, 2001), in an article from the *San Francisco Chronicle (Career),* said, "...listening is a two-way process. Yes, you need to be heard. You also need to hear the other person's ideas, questions, and objections. Being a good listener also means paying attention to content as well as context" (p. W7).

Among the jobs of the middle school counselor is monitoring the behavior and academic success of students. Monitoring means continuous contact with a student and following up with the parents and teachers of that student.

A variety of behaviors can signal the need to help and to bring a middle school student into the purview of the counseling department. Contact might be based on observation of the following:

1. The quiet student who is always alone, who reveals the need for attention
2. The student who does not eat lunch

3. The student whose writing (essays, journal entries) reveals potentially serious problems
4. The student who exhibits anger or meanness
5. The student who bullies others, name calls, and makes threats
6. The student whose grooming and hygiene need attention
7. The student who uses alcohol, tobacco, drugs
8. The student who is obsereved stealing
9. The student who is frequently sent out of the classroom for disruptive behavior
10. The student who has attendance problems
11. The student who seeks attention as a comic but is more disruptive than funny
12. The student whose academic grades have suddenly dropped

Counseling in the middle school is, indeed, serious business. The need to deliver various services—facilitating, consulting, case managing, assisting, supporting, teaching, guiding and counseling, to name a few—to help students enjoy healthy school experiences make middle school counseling an educational priority.

Chapter Three

Perpetual pushing and assurance
put a difficulty out of countenance,
and make a seeming impossibility give way
Jeremy Collier

West Middle School Counseling Department

West Middle School (a fictitious name but a real school) is located in an ethnically diverse urban setting. The student body is largely middle-class. The school is comprised of grades six, seven, and eight. The student population numbers approximately 1,215.

There are two credentialed grade-level counselors. The counseling ratio is approximately 600 to 1. One counselor is responsible for the sixth grade and half of the seventh grade. The other counselor is responsible for the eighth grade and the remaining half of the seventh grade. These counselors follow their counselees from grade six through grade eight.

Besides two grade-level counselors, West Middle School's counseling department includes a head counselor and an assistant principal. Students receive additional support services provided by a part-time school psychologist.

The job of the counselors at West Middle School includes individual counseling, case management, group counseling, teacher-parent-community consultation and coordination. Counselors also participate in the development of activities, the development of guidance curriculum, and site support.

Community resources include medical services, mental health services, social services and law enforcement. Students receive services from the after- school homework program provided by a community based agency staff and after-school tutoring provided by classroom teachers.

Identifying Responsive Services at West Middle School

"Responsiveness" means helping students learn what they should know in order to be successful and learn what they can do to make their school days productive. Responsiveness means helping students understand their own roles in achieving beneficial outcomes.

Middle school counselors spend the majority of their time responding to issues that deal with students' academic success and personal/social adjustment. The day-in-and-day-out focus is on individual needs: how well a student achieves academic expectations; how well a student behaves in different school environments (the classroom, the school yard, the hallway); how well a student gets along with teachers and classmates.

In general, responsive services at West Middle School are planned and coordinated by the head counselor and the grade-level counselor. To maximize student services, the counselor cooperatively employs school-site programs, school district departments, and appropriate community agencies.

On site, the counselors at West Middle School use parent or teacher referrals for Student Success Team (SST) support. The 504 (Section 504 of the Rehabilitation Act of

1973) Plan is used to provide special accommodations for regular students. Beyond the school site, the school district provides services through the Student Attendance Review Board (SARB) to help with attendance problems.

Student referrals are an in-house activity. Students are referred to the counselor for a variety of reasons for example, poor attendance, the breaking of classroom or school rules, the lack of preparation for class, and disruptive behavior. They are also referred for violence, bullying, harassment, health-related problems, and suspected abuse.

Timeliness is extremely important in dealing with referrals. The counselor responds to the referral as quickly as possible. Serious problems are sent to the head counselor or an administrator. Those of less severity are sent to the grade-level counselors.

The counselor's first action in handling such referrals is to clarify the nature of the problem with the teacher who sent the referral and to solicit that teacher's expectations for resolution.

When dealing with student referrals, counselors use different methods and different resources. Some student referrals can be adequately addressed through a one-on-one conference, though it is generally more effective to bolster that with parental involvement. Behavior must be tracked, so that counselors, teachers, and parents see patterns before they become entrenched habits.

If antagonistic behavior is the reason for the student referral, the counselor may use conflict resolution techniques, suggest specific consequences, and use strategies designed to change behavior. Interventions that include those responsible for the student's well-being are most effective. If areas related to a student's physical well-being such as health issues or suspected abuse are the reason for the referral, the counselor must bring together community resources and adequate services to meet that need.

Should there be a problem or situation to which a counselor feels unable to respond, the matter must be immediately referred with explanation to a designated staff member for action.

Some students at West Middle School have the opportunity to receive support through recommendations to the Student Success Team (SST). The SST is an on-site team consisting of the counselor, the student, the student's teachers, the student's parent, an administrator, and may include the school psychologist, the school nurse, and community and district support staff. While any person who works with a student may request an SST, those who most often make requests are parents and teachers.

Pursuant to the SB 65 legislation (Torres, 1985) the SST was developed to assist at-risk students enrolled in California schools implementing the SB 65 School-Based Pupil Motivation and Maintenance Program to achieve academic and personal/social success. In 1991 an independent evaluation of the M&M Program implementation found that the SST process was among the elements that contributed to its success. Based on the SB 65 legislation, the Student Study Team process was codified in the state Education Code (EC 54726b) in 1985.

The mechanics of the SST are handled either by the grade-level counselor, the head counselor or an administrator. The counselor facilitates the conference. An SST meeting is a collaborative effort among all participants—the parents, the student, the teachers, and any other staff (e.g., the school psychologist).

The aim of the SST is to gather information to help the student improve in academic performance and/or behavior. The SST raises concerns, prioritizes suggestions, and designates persons responsible for implementing the suggestions. The SST may determine that a student's chances for improvement require specific adjustments like the modification of the instructional program or mental health assistance or case management. (See SST sample Forms. Printed with written permission from CDE).

Student accountability is the key to a successful outcome. The student is expected to be actively involved in whatever the SST proposes. The counselor manages the recommended areas of student involvement, keeps track of whether the student follows through, and informs all participants of progress.

Contrary to some beliefs, the SST is not a process designed to enroll students in special education services. Rather, the SST is used to assist regular students who demonstrate a need for support in academics or behavior.

Parents of regular students can use the SST process to request specific modifications. The service is rendered through a 504 Plan, which is a resource rooted in Section 504 of the Rehabilitation Act of 1973. It is monitored and enforced by the Office of Civil Rights. Some students are not eligible for special education services, but are deemed disabled. If their disorders or conditions substantially limit their ability to function at school, they are disabled within the meaning of 504, and must be provided the accommodations and special services to benefit from a free and appropriate public education. The district must develop and implement a plan for the delivery of all needed services. (See 504 sample form). Modifications in different areas (environmental, instructional, curricular) can be requested. A parent might even ask for a behavior management plan, increased counseling, or modified testing procedures.

Making the requested modifications a reality for a student require specific steps. First, the counselor arranges an SST conference and discusses the proposed modifications with everyone who has some responsibility for the student. The counselor then completes a "Request for a 504 Form" and forwards the document to the school district for review. If the 504 Request is approved, the counselor completes an Individual Accommodation Plan (IAP) that defines the specific accommodations.

A copy of the IAP is given to the parent (with a copy of the Parent's Rights and Responsibilities), and to the student's teachers. A copy is forwarded to the school district office, and a copy is placed in the student's cumulative folder. Unlike the Special Education Individual Education Plan (IEP), which follows a student from school to school, the 504 IAP is a site-specific service. Once the student leaves the school, the IAP is no longer in effect.

Monitoring a student with attendance problems requires consistent contact, consistent counseling, and consistent follow-up. The Student Attendance Review

Board (SARB) is a referral service that assists the school attendance officer and school counselors in supporting attendance.

Once the counselor or attendance officer notes irregularities in a student's attendance, a student conference is convened. An effort is made to determine why the problem exists, the student is counseled to change the behavior, and the parent is contacted. If the behavior persists, the counselor completes and forwards the appropriate form to the district attendance office for review and follow up.

Chapter Four

I have discovered in life that there are ways
of getting almost anywhere you wan to go,
if you really want to go.

Langston Hughes

Developing the West Middle School Counseling Program

The counseling department staff at West Middle School agreed to incorporate the national counseling standards in their counseling program. This effort involved several steps and a timeline of two to three years.

In order to begin the implementation of the national standards, the counselors at West Middle School, the assistant principal for counseling and the principal began to collaborate in September 2000. They met in an all-day session to review the national counseling standards and the competencies. A slide show on the national standards was presented to the faculty and to the Parent-Teacher-Student Association (PTSA). Opinions were solicited from each group.

The three areas in the national counseling standards are Academic, Personal/Social and Career Development. Each standard specifies the achievement of numerous competencies. Curriculum materials are included in each developmental area.

The counseling staff at West Middle School agreed to implement "Standards A" (including the competencies) of each developmental area—academic, personal/social, and career. (Dahir, Sheldon, & Valiga) pp. 12, 16-17.

Standard A in the academic, personal/social, career areas of the national standards for counseling follow:

The National Standards for Counseling

Academic Development Standard A: Students will acquire attitudes, knowledge, and skills that contribute to effective learning in school and across the life span.

Competency Areas:

1. Improve Academic Self-Concept – Students will:
   - articulate feelings of competence and confidence as learners;
   - display a positive interest in learning;
   - take pride in work and achievement;
   - accept mistakes as essential to the learning process;
   - identify attributes and behaviors, which lead to successful learning

2. Acquire Skills for Improved Learning – Students will:
   - apply time management and task management skills;
   - demonstrate how effort and persistence positively affect learning;
   - use communication skills to know when and how to ask for help when needed;
   - apply knowledge of learning to positively influence school performance

3. Achieve School Success – Students will:

- take responsibility for their own actions;
- demonstrate the ability to work independently, as well as the ability to work cooperatively with other students;
- develop a broad range of interests and abilities
- demonstrate dependability, productivity, and initiative
- share knowledge (Dahir, Sheldon & Valiga) p. 8

Personal/Social Development – Standard A: Students will acquire attitudes, knowledge, and interpersonal skills to help them understand and respect self and others.

Competency Areas:

1. Acquire Self-Knowledge – Students will:
    - develop a positive attitude toward self as a unique and worthy person;
    - identify personal values, attitudes, and beliefs;
    - learn the goal setting process;
    - understand change as a part of growth;
    - identify and express feelings;
    - distinguish between appropriate and inappropriate behaviors;
    - recognize personal boundaries, rights, and privacy needs;
    - understand the need for self-control and how to practice it;
    - demonstrate cooperative behavior in groups;
    - identify personal strengths and assets;
    - identify and discuss changing personal and social roles
    - identify and recognize changing family roles

2. Acquire Interpersonal Skills – Students will:
    - recognize that everyone has rights and responsibilities, including family and friends;
    - respect alternative points of view;

- recognize, accept, respect, and appreciate individual differences;
- recognize, accept, and appreciate ethnic and cultural diversity;
- recognize and respect differences on various family configurations;
- use effective communication skills;
- know that communication involves speaking, listening, and nonverbal behavior;
- learn how to communicate effectively with family;
- learn how to make and keep friends (Dahir, Sheldon, & Valiga). p. 16

Career Development Standard A: Students will acquire the skills to investigate the world of work in relation to knowledge of self and to make informed career decisions.

Competency Areas:

1. Develop Career Awareness – Students will:
   - develop skills to locate, evaluate, and interpret career information;
   - learn about the variety of traditional and nontraditional occupations;
   - development an awareness of personal abilities, skills, interests, and motivations;
   - learn how to interact and work cooperatively in teams;
   - learn to make decisions;
   - learn how to set goals;
   - understand the importance of planning;
   - pursue and develop competency in areas of interest;
   - develop hobbies and avocational interests;
   - learn to balance work and leisure time

2. Develop Employment Readiness – Students will:
    - acquire employability skills such as working on a team, problem solving, and organizational skills;
    - apply job readiness skills to seek employment opportunities;
    - demonstrate knowledge about the changing workplace;
    - learn about the rights and responsibilities of employers and employees;
    - learn to respect individual uniqueness in the workplace;
    - learn how to write a resume;
    - develop a positive attitude toward work and learning;
    - understand the importance of responsibility, dependability, punctuality, integrity, and effort in the workplace;
    - utilize time and task management skills (Dahir, Sheldon & Valiga, p. 12)

Implementing West Middle School Counseling Program

The counseling team at West Middle School began implementation of the national standards in grades six and seven in the fall of 2001. Different methods were used to explain the standards. The assistant principal for counseling services spoke to teachers and students in large groups. There were classroom guidance sessions and individual counseling. Parents were encouraged to discuss the standards at home. The curriculum was designed to enable students to do the following:

1. Set goals
2. Identify the steps in the decision-making process
3. Identify and discuss values

4. Discuss how values influence decisions on handling peer pressure
5. Discuss self-control and the elimination of impulsive behaviors
6. Identify skills that improve learning
7. Accept responsibility for personal actions
8. Manage anger
9. Reduce test anxiety
10. Build interrelationships
11. Demonstrate positive interest in learning
12. Identify the steps in anger management
13. Discuss sexual harassment
14. Understand that learning is a lifelong process

Implementing the counseling standards at West Middle School is the result of continued collaboration and planning. Counselors are able to deliver counseling services in an organized, systematic procedure that supports student achievement.

West Middle School: Assessment and Evaluation

Assessment and evaluation at West Middle School is to be conducted on an annual basis at the end of the fall semester. This time of the school year allows for the availability of both fall and spring grade reports and standardized test results. The assessment and evaluation tools include the following:

1. Report card grades
2. State standardized test scores
3. Student referrals
4. Student suspensions
5. Case studies
6. Teacher Observations
7. Counseling Program Objectives

8. Parent observations

These tools will be used in various case management situations to help students understand their behaviors and learning styles, to develop individual action plans, and to make referrals to outside support services if needed. School grade reports and test scores will be included in the assessment and evaluation of the progress of all students.

West Middle School: Delivering Responsive Services for Academic Development

In accordance with the national counseling standards, the students, the teachers, the parents, and the counselors collaborate on the students' academic preparation, performance, and success. The counselor confers with all students about the need for consistent preparation and reinforces the classroom teachers' expectations. Counselors help students understand what is required of them in a particular class and help them understand the academic requirements of their grade level. To assist students with their academic development, the counselor uses numerous methods of delivery:

1. Individual counseling
2. Action plans
3. Classroom guidance lessons
4. Group counseling
5. Peer mediation
6. Special events/assemblies
7. After-school support services, sports, clubs
8. Community services
9. Parental guidance
10. Parent-teacher conferences
11. Student recognition awards
12. Monitoring student progress (daily, weekly progress reports)
13. Case management
14. Tutorial services
15. Video and print curriculum

Younger middle school students often struggle with simply getting organized and working within a time frame.

When they first enter middle school, they may view everyday procedures as puzzling and overwhelming. The counselor's role is to help by clarifying teacher expectations, recommending strategies for improvement, and encouraging a student's confidence to succeed. Some of the common areas in which counselors provide assistance include:

1. Writing down homework assignments
2. Understanding what an assignment entails
3. Completing homework and class work
4. Keeping track of assignments
5. Turning in assignments on time
6. Understanding the relationship between assignments and grades

These activities guide students to develop and apply organizational skills.

Counselors may use, among other activities, a skill-building curriculum to assist students improve academic performance. There are printed materials and a variety of activities in this curriculum. Among topics addressed might be:

1. How to get organized
2. How to study
3. How to build study skills for academic success
4. How to manage time
5. How to handle test anxiety
6. How to ask for help
7. How to get help (tutorial program)
8. How to handle stress
9. How to handle bogged-down feelings (raise morale)
10. How to develop research skills
11. How to use the Internet

The school counselor maintains a record of the academic performance of his/her counselees. West Middle School uses daily/weekly progress reports and mini-report cards. Students receive daily/weekly progress reports from the counselor and present them to each teacher during the day. The teacher writes a comment or records a letter grade indicating the student's behavior or academic progress for the day or the week. Daily progress reports are given to students who must be monitored on a daily basis for some counselor, teacher, or parental concern. The counselor uses these reports as counseling tools. Students take the reports home for parent signature and return them to the counselor the following day.

A Parent, a student, a teacher, or a counselor may request Progress Reports. The counselor facilitates activities surrounding the progress reports to insure completion and accuracy. The purpose of the reports is to see that a student follows through with classroom requirements on a daily basis: turning in homework, completing assignments, preparing for tests—whatever areas have been identified as needing improvement.

Mini-report cards are school-wide, and are also facilitated by the counseling department. The administrator for counseling prepares and forwards to each homeroom teacher a set of cards with name labels and a class list to prepare the cards for distribution. Students present their mini report cards to each teacher during the day. The last period teacher returns them to the counselor. After checking the cards for completeness, the counselor returns them to the homeroom teachers to distribute for parent's signature. Parents receive grade reports every four and a half weeks.

District report cards are received every nine weeks and mini reports are forwarded home approximately four and a half weeks before and after district reports, thus the every-four-and-a-half-week reports to parents. The grade-level counselors check all mini-cards, pull those that show academic or behavioral problems and counsel those students to change behaviors to enjoy more successful experiences in personal/social and academic areas.

West Middle School: Delivering Responsive Services for Personal/Social Development

> Middle school students are unique. No other grade-span encompasses such a wide range of intellectual, physical, psychological, and social development, and educators must be sensitive to the entire spectrum of these young people's capabilities.
> (California State Department of Education, 1987, p.v)

Students in middle grades have simultaneous needs to be like their peers and yet be different from them. They want their likenesses to be just enough so that others won't think they are "weird" or "uncool." They want their differences to be just enough so as not to look "weird" or "uncool." They want to be one of the group, but they also want their own individual identities.

Middle school students want to be liked, accepted, respected and appreciated, as do most people. But, they may react more dramatically in this pursuit. The school counselor assists students by encouraging them to acquire and to build on the knowledge, skills, and attitudes needed to solve problems, negotiate disputes, prioritize, and set goals. Counseling methods of delivery include the following:

1. Individual counseling
2. Classroom instruction
3. Group counseling
4. Role-playing
5. Parental guidance
6. Individual action plans

Printed materials are available on a number of personal/social developmental topics. West Middle School's counseling department uses these materials on occasion. The printed curriculum includes the following titles:

1. What Young People Should Know About Building Relationships
2. Your Attitude and You
3. Stand Up for Yourself: What Teens Should Know About Peer Pressure
4. Self-Esteem: Respect Yourself
5. Making Decisions: A Guide for Young People
6. Preventing School Violence
7. Going for your Goal: The Key to Reaching Your Potential
8. Stress: What Young People Should Know
9. Let's Talk About Sexual Harassment in School

These discussion topics are timely and interesting to middle school students. Such topics can generate excitement through small group discussions and dramatization.

The following are some strategies school counselors can employ to generate interest and to help students acquire leadership skills, critical thinking skills, and organizational skills:

1. Sharing experiences of positive relationships
2. Discussing types of sexual harassment
3. Role-playing instances of peer pressure
4. Soliciting group ideas for reducing violence in school
5. Making posters on specific topics, post around the school
6. Forming groups to generate activities for keeping the school clean
7. Having school-wide campaigns that demonstrate caring attitudes

Personal/social development is one of the primary goals of the middle school program. Middle school counselors employ various strategies to help students build positive interrelationships, increase academic skills, and enjoy positive experiences.

West Middle School: Delivering Responsive Services for Career Development

Strong academic knowledge, skills, and abilities are the keys to career development. The school counselor teaches students about the need to prepare for careers by educating them about the workplace and the competitive workforce.

Students learn that specialized knowledge, skills, and attitudes are necessary for success. Preparing for a career after high school requires the same rigorous academic courses taken by college-bound students. In today's marketplace, business and industry require a workforce who can read technical manuals, who can solve problems, who are computer literate/trained, and who can work in teams and think on their feet.

While it is unlikely that middle school students will be engaged in career internships or apprenticeships, it is crucial for them to understand the importance of career preparation and the relationship between education and future career goals.

Education is the key to career development and employment success. Students must be encouraged to develop knowledge, attitudes, and skills that enable them to be competitive, productive employees and business owners.

Excellent reading, writing, speaking, thinking, reasoning, analyzing, and computing skills are the gatekeepers to the career marketplace.

Materials, activities, and delivery methods for career development include the following:

1. Career Planning: A Skill for the Future
2. Developing Workplace Skills
3. Writing Your Resume
4. Getting Along on the Job

The counselor uses various activities to engage students and encourage interest in career development. Some activities are among the following:

1. Read newspaper articles for career and employment information
2. Invite guest speakers from business and industry
3. Administer career-aptitude and career-interest inventories
4. Research educational requirements for specific job classifications
5. Group discussions on personal presentation
6. Discussion on knowledge, attitudes, and skills needed for career planning
7. Accompanying parents to work
8. Identify and use resources to locate career information
9. Work place responsibilities
10. Identify preparation and training for current career aspirations

Activities that raise students' awareness and interests about career planning, education and training, and future employment opportunities are among the following:

1. Group projects on projected careers throughout the 21st Century
2. Classroom discussions of job skills in the 21st Century
3. Discuss the types of industries to be in the marketplace in the next 50 years
4. Personal counseling
5. Video presentations
6. Planning and presenting a Career Fair
7. Bringing in guest speakers from various business segments
8. Accompanying parents to work
9. Mock interviews
10. Interviewing business people (gender, age, ethnicity, industry, etc.)

Counselors at West Middle School demonstrate pride in the delivery of counseling services. They deliver responsive services in the academic, the personal/social and the career development areas. Counselors are encouraged to assist and to prepare students to plan their lives to enjoy physical, emotional, spiritual, academic, social, and career growth and development.

Chapter Five

We must nurture our children with confidence. they can't make it if they are constantly told they won't.

George Clements

Suggested Strategies for Delivering Responsive Services for Academic, Personal/Social/ and Career Development

The following suggestions are offered for responsive services related to the national standards. It is further suggested that the counselor employ many different strategies such as those found in printed materials, video, drama, conferences, large group instruction, journal writing, role-playing/dramatizations, and individual and group counseling to help students maximize their potential.

Academic Development

Standard A: Students will acquire attitudes, knowledge, and skills that contribute to effective learning in school and across the life span.

Competency Area: <u>Improve Academic Self-Concept</u>

Students will:

Articulate feelings of competence and confidence as learner

The counselor discusses with students the need to acquire attributes that instill competence and confidence in self.	The counselor and students discuss the need to alter study habits to minimize distractions and maximize retention of content materials.	The counselor helps students plan tasks and accurately complete assignments given by teachers that reflect care, attention, competence, and that increase confidence.

Display a positive interest in learning

The counselor informs students that good study skills result in good grades and demonstrate a positive interest in learning.	The counselor collaborates with teachers to determine students' academic needs, and uses various strategies to engage students in corrective activities to enhance positive interest in learning.	The counselor and students share information on habits, interests, and abilities that facilitate students' learning and demonstrate interest in learning.

Take pride in work and achievement

The counselor encourages students to give their best efforts in all academic preparation.	The counselor discusses the merits of doing one's best in all aspects of education for pride of accomplishment, increased learning, and better grades.	The counselor and students engage in discussions on achievement detailing the fact that success is the result of hard work and persistence.

Accept mistakes as essential to the learning process

The counselor helps students realize and accept that it is human and okay to make mistakes, and it is important to learn from them.	The counselor designs activities for and engages students in discussions that help them evaluate, correct, and accept mistakes as part of learning.	The counselor and students discuss how one learns and benefits from mistakes made in school and across their life span.

Identify attributes and behaviors which lead to successful learning

The counselor talks to students about actions that will help them to be successful learners.	The counselor and students discuss personal characteristics one can count on to help them be successful learners.	The counselor and students engage in discussions that define attributes and behaviors that, when acquired and mastered, will promote successful learning.

Competency Area: Acquire Skills for Improving Learning

Students will:

Apply time management and task management skills

The counselor discusses the need to learn the application of time management and task management.	The counselor and students engage in activities/discussions that focus on learning to and applying amounts of time to work on assignment(s), and maximizing the time allotted for the task(s).	The counselor assists students to learn the importance of time and task management by giving time for specific tasks, and managing the time for maximum effort.

Demonstrate how effort and persistence positively effect learning

The counselor talks with students about the effect of attitude on the learning process.	The counselor engages students in a discussion on how attitude affects effort and persistence in the preparation of learning activities.	The counselor and students discuss attitude toward school and education as a virtue in preparing oneself to receive a good education.

Use communication skills to know when and how to ask for help when needed

The counselor encourages students to communicate with parents, family members, teachers, counselors, friends, and administrators for help.	The counselor encourages students to use communication skills—listening, speaking, reading, and writing—to seek help when needed.	The counselor and students participate in various scenarios of communication to learn when and how to ask for help.

Apply knowledge of learning to positively influence school performance

The counselor discusses learning styles, and elicits information from students about the knowledge of their individual learning styles.	The counselor informs students that knowledge of how they learn will enable them to improve school performance.	The counselor distributes a handout with a list of learning styles with explanations and guides students in discussions (questions and answers) designed to identify their learning style(s), the knowledge of which will positively influence their school performance.

Competency Area: Achieve School Success

Students will:
Take responsibility for their own actions

The counselor impresses upon students being responsible for their actions indicates growth and maturity.	The counselor discusses with students that being responsible for their behavioral acts will result in more positive outcomes.	The counselor and students discuss responsibility, emphasizing that ownership of the behavior belongs to the person expressing it.

Demonstrate the ability to work independently, as well as the ability to work cooperatively with other students

The counselor discusses the importance of being able to work alone as well as being able to work cooperatively with other students. Students Share cooperative group experiences.	The counselor and students discuss the need to be able to work independently (a sign of growth and maturity) and be able to work in groups for shared learning and task management for the benefit of the group.	The counselor and students engage in discussions to facilitate the understanding that working independently and cooperatively begins in the home, continues in school, in the work place, and across their life span.

Develop a broad range of interests and abilities

The counselor encourages students to develop interests and abilities in many areas of life for enjoyment and satisfaction.	The counselor and students discuss the development of various interests and abilities which might affect educational decisions, career choices, or an alternative career.	The counselor and students brainstorm possible outcomes that might result from developing a broad range of interests and abilities, for example, career choice(s), a new body of knowledge, or avocation.

Demonstrate dependability, productivity, and initiative

The counselor encourages students to be dependable and productive, and to initiate activities that require attention and follow up.	The counselor informs students that dependability, productivity and initiative are among the hallmarks of academic success.	The counselor and students explore ways in which demonstrating their dependability, productivity, and initiative have contributed to their academic success and/or that of someone they know.

Share Knowledge

The counselor discusses with students the importance of sharing knowledge, which helps everyone to grow.	The counselor and students discuss the altruism of sharing with others, in which the giver and the receiver profit from the effort.	The counselor and students discuss altruistic deeds. Individuals are asked to share personal acts of altruism, how it affected them, and whether they feel more people should share and help others. One's first opportunity to share begins at home.

Personal/Social Development

Even in social life, it is persistence
which attract confidence more
than talents and accomplishments.

E. P. Whipple

Standard A: Students will acquire attitudes, knowledge, and interpersonal skills to help them understand and respect self and others.

Competency Area: Acquire Self-Knowledge

Students will:

Develop a positive attitude toward self as a unique and worthy person

The counselor helps students see themselves as unique, worthy individuals who give and earn respect.	The counselor plans sessions with students and engages in discussions about the self—positive attitudes, expectations and self-worth.	The counselor engages students in discussions on developing positive self-expectancy.

Identify personal values, attitudes, and beliefs

The counselor engages in self-analysis and assessment of his/her values, attitudes and beliefs to understand better and be able to assist students to clarify and articulate their values.	The counselor assists students in the differentiation among value, belief, and attitude. Students are encouraged to identify, discuss, prioritize, and write at least ten values about self, family, peers and the outside world.	The counselor and students discuss values, attitudes, and beliefs in their relationships, and how these attributes affect choices and decisions.

Learn the goal setting process

The counselor explains and engages students in a discussion on the goal-setting process. The strategy employed is "personalizing." Each student will set a personal goal using these steps. 1) Determine what you want. 2) Write a statement on how it will be achieved. 3) Write a date for achievement. 4) How will you achieve it?	The counselor can use slides to show the steps in the goal-setting process. The significance of each step will be explained. Engage students in the discussion. Discuss the importance of setting short- and long-term goals.	The counselor teaches the importance of setting goals that are within range. Show and discuss examples. Explain the importance of specificity, time, and date in the goal-setting process. Task 1: Each student will write two goals to be discuss at the next session. Task 2: Each student will write an educational, a personal, and a career goal.

Understand change as a part of growth

The counselor discusses with students the concept of change and explains that change is a part of growth—moving on. Engages discussion on changes noticed at home and in the community.	The counselor discusses examples of change, elicits responses from students about change in their lives and ways in which they have been affected by the changes	The counselor explains to students that change is inevitable, as nothing remains the same, and does not always work the way the person would like.

Identify and express feelings

The counselor helps students identify feelings about themselves, and how to appropriately express their feelings.	The counselor informs students that self-expression enhances self-image, and builds and improves oral communication skills.	The counselor engages students in discussions on identifying and expressing feelings to understand and be understood, to help others to see your point of view, and/or seek information.

Distinguish between appropriate and inappropriate behaviors

The counselor uses various strategies to help students differentiate between appropriate and inappropriate behaviors.	The counselor engages students in discussions on the importance of acquiring and demonstrating appropriate behaviors in all relationships.	The counselor assists students to understand, acquire, and demonstrate appropriate behaviors with peers and adults through role playing and/or discussions.

Recognize personal boundaries, rights, and privacy needs

The counselor guides students in the recognition of and respect for boundaries, rights, and privacy needs of self and others.	The counselor helps students to understand and respect personal boundaries, and rights of others through discussion and dialog.	The counselor models and guides students in the recognition, respect, and demonstration of personal boundaries, rights, and privacy needs of others.

Understand the need for self-control and how to practice it

The counselor assists students to acquire techniques for using and understanding self-control.	The counselor discusses the benefits of self-control, and the effects on decisions and personal achievement.	The counselor and students discuss self-control (the quality that leads to self-discipline), and students are encouraged to practice task mastery, keeping commitments, and decision making.

Demonstrate cooperative behavior in groups

The counselor and the students discuss the meaning of cooperation, giving relevant examples	The counselor engages students in discussions and interactions that require cooperation, sharing, and understanding.	The counselor encourages students to recall cooperative situations in the home, in the community and in the classroom, and to evaluate cooperative behavior as it relates to the success of the group.

Identify strengths and assets

The counselor helps students to identify their strengths and assets.	The counselor helps students differentiate between strengths and assets in different situa tions and areas.	The counselor helps students identify, understand, differentiate, and assess strengths and assets.

Identify and discuss changing personal and social roles

The counselor discusses social roles in the family, among peers, at school, and in social groups.	The counselor and students discuss personal and social roles at different stages in life – childhood, adolescence, young adult, adult, and senior.	The counselor and students discuss and role play personal and social roles at various stages of life to understand how and why roles change.

Identify and recognize changing family roles

The counselor discusses changing roles in families, and give some reasons for changes.	The counselor and students engage in discussions about the roles of various family members.	The counselor and students discuss the identification of roles of various family members and note when, how, and why their roles change.

Competency Area: <u>Acquire interpersonal skills</u>

Students will:

Recognize that everyone has rights and responsibilities, especially, including family and friends

The counselor helps students recognize and discuss human rights and responsibilities. Emphasize that respon sibilities are as important as rights.	The counselor and students engage in discussions that focus on the understanding that rights are exercised with responsibility.	The counselor and students engage in discussions that reinforce the moral law that rights have corresponding responsibilities for everyone, including family and friends.

Respect alternative points of view

The counselor informs students of the necessity to respect others' points of view, and expect respect in return.	The counselor and students discuss the need to see things through the eyes of others, which encourages understanding and respecting various points of view.	The counselor sets up activities that include active participation of students—oral and/or written focusing on points of view.

Recognize, accept, respect, and appreciate individual difference

The counselor models these characteristics in interacting with students, colleagues, and parents.	The counselor engages the students in discussions on individual differences, how they relate to those differences, and how those differences have impacted their lives.	The counselor and students discuss situations associated with communal relationships, which are rooted in recognizing, accepting, and appreciating individual differences while building relationships on likenesses.

Recognize, accept, and appreciate ethnic and cultural diversity

The counselor models these characteristics in interacting with students, colleagues, parents, and the public.	The counselor helps students understand that recognition, acceptance, and appreciation for ethnic and cultural diversity enriches the lives of everyone by reducing tensions; sharing cultural and educational information; planning community activities; giving communal support; and developing relationships.	The counselor and students discuss experiences related to ethnic and cultural activities describing personal behaviors, relationships, and the effects these interactions have had on lives.

Use effective communication skills

The counselor plans, designs, and engages students in activities that complement the classroom teacher's instruction on communication skills.	The counselor uses small or large group instruction to actively engage students in discussions on forms of communication—speaking, listening, writing, and nonverbal behavior.	The counselor and students engage in large group (classroom) activities that include roleplaying scenarios on speaking, listening, and nonverbal behavior—to learn to communicate effectively.

Learn how to make and keep friends

The counselor and student discuss friendship and what it means to have friends.	The counselor and students brainstorm aspects of friendship with emphasis on being a friend, having a friend, and nurturing the relationship.	The counselor and students engage in discussions on the expectations of friends, for example, how to recognize potential problems in relationships, characteristics of lasting friends, and what to do when friendships break up.

Career Development

The greatest asset of any nation is the spirit of its people, and the greatest danger that can menace any nation is the break down of its spirit—the will to win and the courage to work.

George B. Cartelyou

Standard A: Students will acquire the skills to investigate the world of work in relation to knowledge of self and to make informed career decisions.

Competency Area: Develop Career Awareness

Students will:

Develop skills to locate, evaluate and interpret career information

The counselor engages students in a discussion about careers. He/she begins by eliciting responses to several questions: What is a job? What is work? What is employment? What is a career? As the discussion continues, they discuss careers of people they know including family members.	The counselor and the students discuss sources for finding career information. They visit the school library where they Look up career information in the Occupation Outlook Handbook, the Dictionary of Occupational Titles, the newspaper, and the Internet.	The counselor and the students discuss job categories, the longevity of job types, evaluation of job types for career interests, and career information in relation to education, skills and abilities.

Learn about the variety of traditional and nontraditional occupations

The counselor and the students discuss the meanings of the terms "traditional" and "nontraditional." The counselor asks students to name careers of parents, family members, and other people they know, and explain whether their careers are "traditional" or "nontraditional."	The counselor and the students engage in a discussion on the longevity of traditional and nontraditional careers occupations.	The counselor asks students to list four occupations—two traditional and two nontraditional—and explain the reasons for their choices. Use the DOT, OOH, GOE, EDD, and the Internet to research these occupations.

Develop an awareness of personal abilities, skills, interests, and motivations

The counselor begins the discussion by asking students to give a description and an example of ability, a skill, an interest, and a motivation. The counselor completes the task if students do not give accurate information.	The counselor asks the students to get in groups of two or three and identify these traits in each other. A student will record during the discussions, and report to the whole group. The counselor asks, "Who observed these traits in himself or herself?"	The counselor and the students engage in discussion on the benefits of being aware of or knowing one's personal traits in relation to career awareness.

Learn how to interact and work cooperatively in teams

The counselor begins a discussion on "team work." He/she engages students in the discussion by asking who is, or has been, an active member on a team. They continue the discussion on cooperation, give-and-take, and how the team maintains its strength.	The counselor asks: What are some ways one can be cooperative member of a team? What are some ways to ensure success of the team? The dis-cussion continues with the importance of each team member performing assigned tasks and assisting others.	The counselor gives the students the task of comparing the interaction and cooperation of members on an employment team to the interaction and cooperation of members on a sports team.

Learn to make decisions

The counselor first informs students that one makes decisions based on one's values. He/she asks: What are values? The counselor might distribute printed materials on values, and engage student in a developmental reading activity with discussions.	The counselor might ask: Where do we get our values? When are values formed? After counselor-student interactions, the counselor might continue with the following explanations: We get our values from parents, teachers, counselors, ministers, coaches, past experiences, and society. However, what we choose to value is up us. Our values are formed during growth and development.	The counselor informs the students that decision-making is a step-by-step process. Discussion: 1) Identify the problem or situation. 2) Think of all the possible actions you can take. 3) Gather information. 4) Consider possible consequences. 5) Make a choice. 6) Take action. The counselor explains that after one takes action, he/she must be ready to take responsibility for the action.

Understand the Importance of Planning

The counselor begins the discussion with the question: Why is it necessary to make—plans to complete certain tasks? After counselor-student discussions, the counselor explains. Planning is necessary because it sets up a course of action that will help the person move and work toward the goal. The counselor and the students discuss situations for which a plan was necessary.	The counselor engages students in the discussion by first informing them that there is a process for planning similar to the process of setting goals. (After all, setting goals is planning). The counselor asks student to list three steps in the planning process. Discussion follows. The counselor explains that there is a difference between a planning and dreaming.	The counselor discusses how a *plan* differs from a *dream*. Quoting from NAIC Investing for Life … Teenagers. (1997). pp. 6 & 7. The dream generates thoughts. The plan puts the thoughts into actions. Process: 1) Set goals. 2) Acquire knowledge. 3) generate alternatives. 4) Develop a strategy. Show commitment. Be flexible. Plans can be changed.

Pursue and develop competency in areas of interest

The counselor and the students discuss educational preparation for areas of interest—sourses that help develop competency in those areas.	The counselor encourages students to research areas of interest, and take courses that meet requirements for a wide variety of career choices.	The counselor and the students discuss areas of interest that might become a vocation or an avocation. Task: The counselor asks students to list areas of interest and brainstorm preparation requirements.

Learn to balance work and leisure time

Discussions on balancing work and leisure time permits the counselor and the students to explore leisure activities that might be pursued and developed into careers.	The counselor elicits responses from individual students about hobbies and recreations, (and other leisure activities) and the merits of turning them into careers.	The counselor and the students discuss reasons for learning to balance work and leisure time. Students are asked to give examples of balancing work and leisure time.

Competency Area: Develop Employment Readiness

Students will:

Acquire employability skills such as working on teams, problem solving and organizational skills

The counselor engages students in a discussion on and explains how teamwork, organizational skills, and problems solving, relate to employment readiness. Watch a video on job readiness.	The counselor and the students explore current skills needed for these areas. The students discuss the extent to which they need to develop skills for employment readiness when they enter the work place.	The counselor and the students discuss what needs to occur to develop skills for employment readiness. Task: List at least five empoyment skills and tell how you will develop them for employment readiness.

Apply job readiness skills to seek employment opportunities

The counselor asks the question, "What does job readiness mean to you?" After discussion about job readiness, the counselor tells the students the following: First and foremost, it means being able to read and comprehend; having good math skills; being able to communicate effectively; and it means knowing how to work.	Job readiness is interesting to the students. They and the counselor continue the discussion. The counselor informs them of other considerations for job readiness—having a positive attitude; being able to take risks; having faith in one's skills and abilities; showing initiative; and personal presentation.	As the counselor continues the discussion on employment readiness, students learn that the following characteristics are also essential in situations other than employment: dependability, responsibility, punctuality, integrity, and effort. Task. Write a one-page essay describing your job-readiness skills.

Demonstrate knowledge about the changing workplace

The counselor explains to the students what is meant by the changing workplace. He/she discusses changes in the work-place in relation to current employment trends.	The counselor talks about the culture of the workplace. Some are product oriented. Some are client/customer oriented. Some have relaxed dress code and flexible hours. Task: Talk to parent, relatives, family friends about changes and culture in the workplace. Project the changes that will likely be in effect when you enter the workplace.	The workplace discussion continues. The counselor informs students that fewer workplaces have a 40-hr. work week. Many have longer hours. Some workplaces have a four-day workweek. Some have telecommuting. Task: research the changing workplace. Be able to list five things that are changing in the workplace.

Learn about the rights and responsibilities of employers and employees

The counselor reminds the students of their rights and responsibilities saying, "In the school setting, the Student Handbook spells out your rights and responsibilities. Employers and employees have rights and responsibilities in the work place. For example, you have the right to a 30-minute lunch period. You have the responsibility to adhere to that time.	Students are encouraged to list as many rights and responsibilities in the workplace as possible. The counselor informs students that for every right there is a responsibility.	The counselor and the students will view a video on workplace rights and responsibilities. The counselor asks, "Would you add or delete any of the rights and responsibilities shown in the video?" Why? Why not? Group discussion follows.

Learn to respect individual uniqueness in the workplace

The counselor engages the students in a discussion on the unique characteristics that are beneficial in the workplace. For example, Jane and Susan are self-starters. They see what needs to be done and do it without expecting to receive special treatments. They willingly assist co-workers. They appreciate and take advantage of trust from others. The students are asked to identify something unique about each other.	The counselor asks students to discuss some particular uniqueness they have observed in friends, family, teachers, or counselor.	Task: Write a half-page essay describing your respect for individual uniqueness. Sharing: The counselor asks students to share their appreciation for the uniqueness observed in others.

Learn how to write a résumé

The counselor explains the meaning of the résumé and why it is used in the job process. He/she shares copies with students so that they can study the contents of what it should and should not contain.	The counselor engages students in a discussion about résumé writing by asking what necessary items should be included.	Prior to writing the draft of a résumé, the counselor instructs students to list in chronological order the items they will include in a résumé. When the list is complete, write the first draft.

Develop a positive attitude toward work and learning

The counselor informs the students that a positive attitude in any setting produces a more positive atmosphere. The counselor continues to discuss behavior—feeling, thinking, and acting toward something or someone. Attitudes and behaviors of employers and employees determine the culture of the workplace.	A discussion among the students and the counselor on the affect of attitude toward work reveals that a positive attitude in the workplace affects fellow employees, employers, and oneself. Think of instances when you have been in the presence of someone with a negative attitude. Discuss the atmosphere that is generated.	The counselor asks the students to list, for discussion, at least five positive attitudes toward work and learning that promote harmony in the workplace.

References

Bennett, L. B. (2000). Doctoral Dissertation. *Self-perceptions of support for the professional role of speech and language pathologists in public school settings.* (Doctoral Dissertation, University of San Francisco, 1999). Doctoral Abstract International, Vol. 60-10. 99-50318. p. 149

California State Department of Education. (1987. Caught in the middle: Educational reform for young adolescents in California public schools. *Sacramento, CA: Author.*

California State Department of Education. (2001). *Taking center stage: A commitment to standards-based education for California's middle grade students.* Sacramento, CA: Author.

Campbell, C. A., & Dahir, C. A. (1997). *Sharing the vision: The national standards for school counseling programs.* Alexandria, VA: American School Counselor Association.

Dahir, C. A., Sheldon, C. B., & Valiga, M. J. (1998). *Vision into action: Implementing the national standards for school counseling programs.* Alexandria, VA: American School Counselor Association.

Krumboltz, J. D. (1966). *Stating the goals of counseling.* Fullerton, CA: California Personnel and Guidance Association.

Lapan, R. T., Gysbers, N. C., & Petroski, G. F. (Summer, 2001) *Helping seventh graders be safe and Successful: A statewide study of the impact of comprehensive guidance and counseling Programs.* Alexandria, VA: Journal of Counseling and Development. American Counseling Association. Vol. 79-3

Lipson, J. G., Dibble, S. L. & Minarik, P. A. (1998). *Culture & nursing care: A pocket guide.*

School of Nursing. UCSF Nursing Press. San Francisco, CA:

Mackay, Harvey. (2001), June. *Listening is easy, good listening requires effort.* San Francisco Chronicle. San Francisco, CA.

Investment Education Institute (The) & the National Association of Investors Corporation. (1997). *Investing for life: A simplified guide to the complex world of investments and personal finance for teenagers.* Madison Heights, MI:

Reynolds, William M. (1987). *About me. Reynolds adolescent depression scale.* Form HS.
Psychological Assessment Resources, Inc. Odessa, FL:

Ruggiero, V. R. (2000, Summer). *Bad behavior: Confronting the views that hinder students' learning.* American Educator. Washington, DC: American Federation of Teachers.

Shaw, J. E. (2000). *Jack and Jill, why they kill.* Seattle, WA: Onjinjinkta Publishing.

Trujillo, F. X. (1998). A Teacher Is. [Brochure] Sacramento, CA: ProTeach.

Suggested Readings

American School Counselor Association. (1990. *Role of the school counselor.* Alexandria, VA: ASCA Press.

American School Counselor Association. (1994, June). (Position statement: *The emerging role of* the *school counselor.* ASCA Counselor, 31 (5), 7.

American School Counselor Association. (1997). *The national standards for school counseling programs.* [Brochure] [On-line]. Available: www.schoolcounselor.org/national.htm

Arredondo, P., Toporek, P., Brown, S., Jones, J., Locke, D. C., Sanchez, J., & Stadler, H. (1966). *Operationalization of the multicultural counseling competencies.* Alexander, VA: Association for Multicultural Counseling and Development.

Blacher, J. H., Murray-Ward, M., & Uellendahl, G. E. (2000). *School counselors' use of assessment and its relationship to their training.* CACD Journal, 20, 21-26.

California State Department of Education. (2001). *Taking center stage: A commitment to Standards-based education for California's middle grade students.* Sacramento, CA: Author.

Delpit, L. (1995). *Other people's children: Cultural conflict in the classroom.* New York, NY: New Press.

Ladson-Billings, G. (1994). *The dreamkeepers:* Successful *teachers of African American children.* San Francisco, CA: Josey-Bass.

Monroe, L., (1999). *Nothing's impossible: Leadership lessons from inside and outside the classroom.* New York, NY: Public Affairs.

National Council on Educating Black Children. (1986). *A blueprint for action.* Silver Spring, MD: Author.

Rosemond, J. K. (2001, February). *Feeling good, acting bad.* Hemispheres. Greensboro, NC: Pace Communications.

Teaching Tolerance. (1999). *Responding to hate at school: A guide for teachers, counselors, and administrators.* [Brochure] Montgomery, Al: The Southern Poverty Law Center. Author.

Teaching Tolerance. (1999) *A place at the table: History and identity through the eyes of today's youth.* [Video] Montgomery, Al: The Southern Poverty Law Center. Author.

Wynn, M. (1998). *The eagles who thought they were chickens: A tale of discovery.* Marietta, GA:

STANDARDS-BASED COUNSELING IN THE MIDDLE SCHOOL

Order Form

Name____
Institution_____________________________________
Address______________________________________
City_State_Zip__________________________________
Day Phone (__)__________Evening Phone (__)__________
Fax:____
Email:____

Ship To (No P. O. Boxes)__________________________
Name____
Address______________________________________
City State____________________Zip ________________

Price $_______________________________________
copies at_=___________________________________
Tax____
Shipping and Handling____________________________
Total Amount $_________________________________
Call regarding discounts for orders of multiple copies.________
MC #_Expiration Date_____________________________
VISA #_Expiration Date___________________________

Signature______________________________________
Send Order Form to:_______________________________

California Association for Counseling and Development
2555 E. Chapman Street, Suite 201
Fullerton, CA 92831

Phone: 714 871-6460 Fax: 714 871-5132 Email: cacd@cacd.org
www.cacd.org

SST SUMMARY FORM

STUDENT: ________ **SCHOOL:** ________ **TEAM:** ________ **DATE OF INTIAL SET:** ________

PRIMARY LANGUAGE: ________ **GRADE:** ____ **BIRTHDATE:** ______ **PARENTS:** ________

STRENGTHS	KNOWN Information	KNOWN Modifications	CONCERNS Prioritize	QUESTIONS	STRATEGIES Brainstorm	ACTIONS (Prioritize)	Who	When
				DESIRED STUDENTS OUTCOMES			AS EVIDENCED BY Method of measuring Progress	

Follow Up Date: ________ ***Invite:*** ________

Team Member's Signature/Position

1. Parents________
2. Student________
3. Administrator________
4. Referring Teacher________
5. ________/________
6. ________/________
7. ________/________
8. ________/________

SST FOLLOW UP FORM

STUDENT: ______ **SCHOOL:** ______ **TEAM:** ______ **DATE OF INITIAL SST:** ______
TODAYS DATE: ______
PRIMARY LANGUAGE: ______ **GRADE:** ______ **BIRTHDATE:** ______ **PARENTS:** ______

NEW INFORMATION	PREVIOUS ACTIONS	OUTCOMES	NEW ACTIONS	Who	When
			DESIRED STUDENTS OUTCOMES	AS EVIDENCED BY Method of measuring Progress	

Follow Up Date: ______ ***Invite:*** ______

Team Member's Signature/Position:

1. Parent ______ 5. ______/______
2. Student ______ 6. ______/______
3. Administraror ______ 7. ______/______
4. Referring Teacher ______ 8. ______/______

STUDENT STUDY TEAM (SST) LOG FORM 1

Log Dates from ________ to ________

____
Contact Person Responsible for Maintaining Log

____
School School No.

	Student Name	Referral Source	Birth Date	Ethnic	Date SST Referral	Type of Referral	Date SST Mtg. #1	Outcome See Legend	Date SST Mtg. #2	Outcome	Comments
1.											
2.											
3.											
4.											
5.											
6.											
7.											
8.											
9.											
10.											
11.											
12.											

A. Stop - resolved
B. Transferred or withdrawn
C. Develop/use a support system in the school
D. Develop/use a support systems with community assistance
E. District Resources/Alternatives outside the school site
F. Referred for Special Program assessment, determination of eligibility; specify program
G. Other, specify in Comment box

Type of Referral: Attendance, Behavior
Academic, Other, etc.

REQUEST FOR 504 PLAN

Student ______________ Grade ______ Date of Birth ______________
Date ______________ School ______________
504 Coordinator ______________ Telephone ______________
Parent/Guardian ______________ Telephone ______________
Address ______________ Zip code ______________

Reason for 504 Plan (Please describe student's diagnosis, medications, physical impairment, health needs, learning difficulties, etc.)

What strategies are currently in place at school?

What modifications are being proposed? Additional funds needed and amount?

Name of physician, psychologists, school personnel, or others involved in the case and short summery of their impressions. (If medical diagnosis, must have physician's letter, medical orders and signed medication form.)

Who initiated 504 plan? _____ School _________ parent/guardian

Did parent/guardian provide consent for conderation of eligibility (writing plan)?

(For 504 Dictrict Committee's Use)

DISPOSITION
_____ 504 Plan is needed _____ 504 Plan is not needed. (See comments below)
_____ 504 School Committee to write Individual Accommodation Plan _____ Pupil Services input will be needed to write Individual Accommodation Plan

COMMENTS

Approved by: ______________

Please complete this form to secure premission for your School Committee to develop the 504 Plan for any student.

Section 504 Service Plan

Date: ____________________
Location of meeting: ________________________________

Student and Parent Information

Student:__________________ Birth Date: ____________ Sex: _______ Grade: ________
Address: ____
Street City State Zip
School of Attendance: _________________ School of Residence: __________________
Parent/Guardian: __________________ Home Phone: _________ Work Phone: ___________

Present level of performance:
Summarize present levels of performance areas. Include/identify outside assessment information. Indicate strengths and weaknesses. This summary shall be descriptive of the student as a handi-capped person as defined by Section 504 Regulation 104.30*

Check if assessed.
___1. Caring for self ____
___2. Performing manual task____
___3. Walking ____
___4. Hearing ____
___5. Speaking ____
___6. Breathing ____
___7. Learning ____
___8. Working ____
____

ELIGIBILITY FOR SERVICES UNDER SECTION 504
_______Student meets eligibility requirements under Section 504 definitions.
_______Student does not meet eligibility requirements under Section 504 definitions.
_______Rationale for above determination:
____

Regulation 104.30 states:
"Disabled person" means any person who (i) has a physical impairment, which substantially limits one or more major life activities, (ii) has a record of such impairment, or (iii) is regarded as having such impairment.

As used in paragraph 0) of this section, the phrase:
(i) **"Physical or mental impairment"** means (A) any physiological disorder or condition, cosmetic disfigurement, or anatomical loss affecting one or more of the following systems: neurological; musculoskeletal; special sense organs; respiratory, including speech organs; cardiovascular; reproductive; digestive; genito-urinary; hermic and lymphatic; skin; and endocrine; or (B) any mental or psychological disorder, such as mental retardation; organic brain syndrome, emotional or mental illness, or specific learning disabilities.

(ii) **"Major life activities"** means functions such as caring for one's self, performing manual tasks, walking, seeing, hearing, speaking, breathing, substantially learning, or working.

(iii) **"Has a record of such an impairment"** means has a history of, or has been misclassified as having a mental or physical impairment that limits one or more major life activities.
(iv) **"Is regarded as having an impairment"** means (A) has a physical or mental impairment that does not substantially limit major life activities, but is treated by recipient as constituting such a limitation: (B) has a physical or mental impairment that substantially limits major life activities only as a result of the attitudes of others toward such impairment; or (C) has none of the impairments defined in paragraph 0) (1) (2) (3) of this section but is treated by a recipient as having such impairment.

504 SERVICES AS NEEDED

TYPE	Frequency	Duration: Min. Per.	Begin: Month/Year	End: Month/Year
Regular Education Services				
Health Services				
Other				

PARENT DECISION/SIGNATURES

I agree with services as noted above.

I do not agree with services as noted above and understand that I have a right to request a **Section 504 Complaint Hearing** by writing the complaint to the Superintendent of Schools.

Parent Signature ______________________________ Date ____________

SIGNATURES OF OTHER PARTICIPANTS

Administrator/Designee ______________________________ Date____________

Teachers ______________________________ Date____________

______________________________ ____________

Student ______________________________ Date____________

Other ______________________________ Date____________
Title ______________________________

Site administrator retain a copy. Send a copy to District Section 504 Coordinator.

Section 504 Plan for ________ School for 2001 - 2002

	Last Name	First Name	Grade	Impairment	School for Fall 2001	Date of last Plan
1						
2						
3						
4						
5						
6						
7						
8						
9						
10						

Notes:

Notes:

Notes:

Notes:

Notes:

Notes:

Notes:

Notes:

Notes:

Notes:

Notes:

Notes:

ABOUT THE AUTHOR

Mary Ellen Davis has worked in education and counseling for thirty-seven years. She began her teaching career in the New York City Schools. She accepted a teaching position in the San Francisco Schools in 1968, where she taught high school for eleven years. Mary Ellen received the master's degree and the Pupil Personnel Services Credentials from San Francisco State University. Her counseling career began in 1979. She received the School Administration Credential from California State University, Hayward. Mary Ellen currently holds the position of assistant principal of counseling services at the middle school level. She is currently president of the California Association for Counseling and Development (CACD) a state branch of the American Counseling Association (ACA).

Printed in the United States
123265LV00004B/214/A

9 781403 310873